D

How to Build an Underground Shelter in Your Home and Protect Your Family

John Becker

ISBN: 9781073551484

Table of contents

A. Preparing Pressure- and radiation-proof protective shelters

1. Introduction

With the publication of this training material we pursue the goal of achieving a certain protection of the population against the consequences of an air attack within a short period of time. This will be possible if every citizen himself actively helps to prepare protective cellars in the existing buildings. But willingness alone is not enough to solve this task. This brochure is intended to convey some knowledge.

Part A explains how the pressure- and radiation-safe protective cellars in the existing buildings of cities are to be prepared, while Part B deals with the preparation of radiation-safe protective cellars.

After familiarizing oneself with the definitions, the reader is given a brief explanation of the effects against which a protective cellar offers protection in the event of an air attack and of the stresses that occur during such an attack. For the selection of suitable rooms for the extension of a protective cellar, however, the following basic requirements and points of view are also important. Detailed instructions on how to carry out the extension and what the technical equipment must be like naturally occupy the largest space. Numerous construction drawings and sketches enable the reader to understand the necessary measures even better. Finally, this booklet contains an overview of the equipment of a shelter for 40 persons.

If none of the variants described here can be applied to the local conditions, an expert should be consulted. His recommendations for the selection of suitable rooms will certainly be useful. The evaluation of the ceilings should, however, always be carried out by him.

The dimensions and specifications in the construction drawings refer to the load assumptions dealt with in Section 3. In the case of basements to be built inside buildings, the load values should be taken from Figure 1a. If, on the other hand, the position of a protective cellar corresponds to the situations shown in Figures 1b and 1c, the dimensions of the bracing elements must be recalculated using the usual dimension tables. (The increased permissible stresses of the valid guidelines for air-raid protection structures must be taken into account).

Thus, this training material should fulfil its purpose to provide you with the necessary equipment for the preparation of air-raid shelters.

For all following drawings:

1m = 3,28 feet
1cm = 0,3937 inch

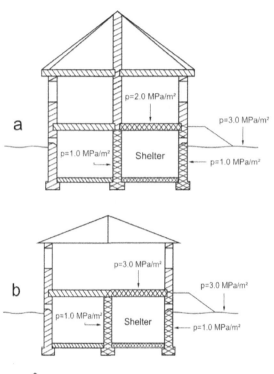

a

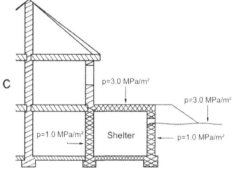

b

c

Fig. 1: Load of a protective cellar by the pressure wave

(a) in the presence of at least one upper floor ceiling and one roof covering,
(b) if there is only one roof covering,
(c) if the protective cellar is located in a cellar area outside the perimeter walls of the building

2. Definitions

The following sections contain a number of terms, the meaning of which will be briefly explained here before.

A **protective ceiling** is an existing ceiling or cellar ceiling reinforced by constructive measures, which is to be prepared according to the scope of protection required in Section 3.

Protective walls are the enclosure components of a protective cellar which are reinforced according to their protective function or specially built for this purpose and must withstand the loads according to Section 3.

An **emergency outlet** is used to leave the protective cellar if the normal entrance or exit is buried. It normally consists of a **horizontal creeper** and a **vertical emergency exit**.

The **sluice** of a protective cellar is closed to the outside by a gas-tight pressure door and to the living room by a gas-tight door. The **gas-tight pressure door** must withstand an air pressure corresponding to the degree of protection and at the same time be gas-tight. The **gas-tight** door should hermetically seal the protective cellar (lounge) from the outside air.

3. Scope of protection and load assumptions

Cellar rooms, which are developed after the principles and notes explained here, offer protection from

- the pressure wave generated by a nuclear weapon detonation, which generates a maximum pressure of 3.0 MPa/m^2 in the area of the structure on the earth's surface.
  In the static calculation, the calculated load on the protective ceiling should only be assumed to be p = 2.0 MPa/m^2 if there are other ceilings above the protective ceiling, but at least one upper storey ceiling and one roof covering. The horizontal load on the basement walls must be assumed to be p = 1.0 MPa/m^2 as the static load (see Fig. 1a-c).
  If there is no other ceiling above the protective ceiling to be prepared, the calculated load of the protective ceiling must be assumed to be 3.0 MPa/m^2;

- the debris loads acting on the cellar ceiling as a result of the collapse of the parts of the building above. They are to be assumed as static loads of 2.0 MPa/m^2;

- the heat radiation of the assumed nuclear weapon detonation;

- the effect of chemical, radiological and biological agents of attack.

A load of 3.0 MPa/m^2 must be assumed for gas-tight pressure doors, irrespective of the specifications in this training material. The equipment and equipment of the protective cellar must be such as to guarantee the persons seeking protection a safe stay for a period of approximately 6 days.

4. Selection of suitable rooms

The protective cellar to be installed should contain the rooms and installations shown in Figures 24 or 25. If the required room sizes are to be determined, the following basic requirements must be taken as a basis:

- A floor area of at least 0.6 m² per person and an airspace of at least 1.5 m³ must be provided in the recreation room;

- a maximum of 40 persons shall be accommodated in a lounge and a total of no more than 80 persons in a shelter;

- the lock shall have a floor area of at least 1,00 m X 1,40 m, and

- for a dry lavatory a dry lavatory of at least 0.80 m X 1.00 m is required.

The following aspects must be taken into account when selecting the cellar rooms to be extended:

1. the distance between the location of the person seeking protection and the protective cellar should not be more than 200 m and the way there should be as splinter-proof as possible.

2. the protective cellars should not be located near the corners of the building or under wooden beam ceilings.

3. rooms are to be preferred as protective cellars, whose ceilings and walls are not plastered and which have as few openings as possible (windows and doors) as well as openings (pipe penetrations, chimney cleaning flaps etc.).

4. the occupants of the protective cellar must not be additionally endangered by flammable or toxic materials, supply lines (gas, steam heating and main water lines, sleeves of high-voltage cables) or by possibly falling large individual loads.

5. the external walls of the rooms above the protective cellar should not have any larger openings (shop windows, larger doors, etc.).

6. the lower edge of the cellar ceiling should be as low as possible, but not higher than 1.00 m above the site.

7. the external walls of protective cellars with a protective ceiling above the site must be reinforced by earth fillings or other measures. Terraces, open stairs and the like must be used as existing reinforcements.

8. the surrounding walls of the protective cellar must be at least 36.5 cm thick on the outside of the building and at least 24 cm thick inside the building.

9. the free wall length of the external walls should not exceed the values specified in section 5.11. The free wall length of the external walls should not exceed the values specified in section 5.11.

10. the emergency exit shall be as far away from the entrance as possible and shall be positioned so as to ensure good natural ventilation of the basement.

11. the minimum distance to the nearest protective cellar shall generally be 30 m. If two protective cellars are directly adjacent to each other, both protective cellars must be separated by a load-bearing wall (same thickness as the surrounding walls) and connected with two gastight pressure doors (see Fig. 2).

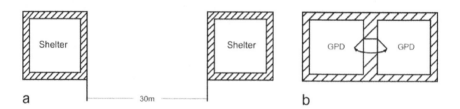

Fig. 2: *Position of protective cellars in relation to each other*
(a) Minimum distance between two adjacent protective cellars.
(b) If two protective cellars are adjacent to each other, the partition wall shall be of the same thickness as the other enclosure components. The opening in the partition shall be closed by two gastight pressure doors (GPD).

5. Expansion measures

5.1 Reinforcement measures on the perimeter walls of protective cellars

5.1.1 Free wall length

The term free wall length refers to the length of a wall between bracings by walls, masonry supports or wooden constructions. The following free wall lengths must not be exceeded for external walls of buildings as enclosing walls of protective basements:

a) In buildings consisting only of ground floor and attic, wall thicknesses up to 36.5 cm = 2.50 m;

b) in buildings consisting of ground, upper and attic floors for non-ceiling walls with thicknesses up to 36.5 cm = 2.50 m and

c) for all multi-storey buildings and for the cases mentioned under a) and b) for wall thicknesses over 36.5 cm = 5.00 m.

The following free wall lengths are permissible for interior walls of buildings as enclosing walls of protective cellars:

a) For ceiling-bearing interior walls = 5.00 m;

b) non-ceiling interior walls must be at least 24 cm thick. The free wall length may not exceed 5.00 m if the walls are not exposed to direct pressure (e.g. if the basement windows of the adjacent rooms are sealed) and 2.50 m if the adjacent rooms are not sealed.
The free wall length can be reduced by additional bracing (partition walls, pier templates, wooden bracing).

5.1.2 Bracing by masonry pier supports

Pillar templates have dimensions of 50 x 50 cm. They are made of bricks in lime-cement mortar, fully grouted and suitable for dressing. Before this, every second brick layer of the existing wall must be provided with 6 to 8 cm deep slits (in pillar width). When bricking up the pier template, the bricks are pushed into these slots and thus interlocked with the wall. If the ceiling has steel girders or concrete beams, the piers must be arranged in such a way that they additionally support them.

A pillar may be placed directly on the solid basement floor if it is still in good condition and is not hollow. Whether the floor is hollow or not can be determined by a knock test (by hammering with a hammer). If the floor is hollow, it must be chiseled, the soil tamped down and the pillar bricked up from there.

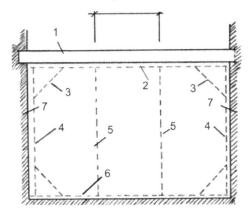

Distance between props
according to section 5.2

System of bracing

Corner formation of the frame

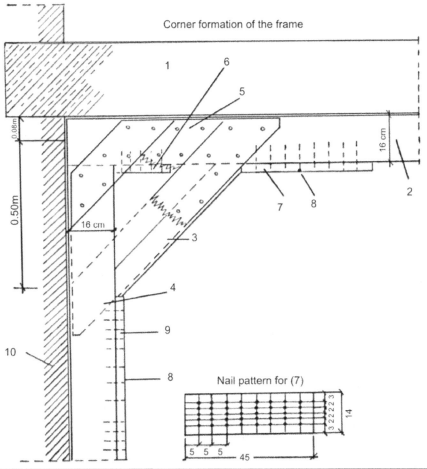

0.08m

16 cm

0.50m

16 cm

16 cm

Nail pattern for (7)

14

3 2 2 2 2 3

5   5   5

45

Frame for vertical wall bracing

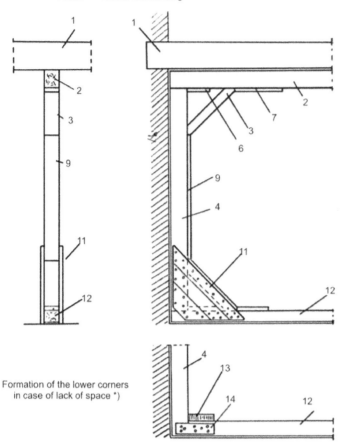

Formation of the lower corners
in case of lack of space *)

Fig. 3: Vertical wall bracing
bracing system: **1.** Ceiling, **2.** beam, **3.** headband, **4.** wall timber, **5.** support, **6.** threshold, **7.** wall to be braced

Corner formation of the frame and frame for vertical wall bracing: **1.** ceiling, **2.** beam 14/16 of the ceiling bracing is used for wall bracing (spacing of the supports according to section 5.2), **3.** headband 8/14, **4.** wall timber 14/16, **5.** boarding on both sides with 4 nails each 10 cm long, **6.** Board 3/14 20 cm long with 10 nails 10 cm long, **7.** Board 3/14 45 cm long, **8.** 40 nails 10 cm long, **9.** Board 3/14 between upper and lower headband, **10.** wall to be stiffened, **11.** headband and boarding on both sides at all corners, **12.** threshold 14/10, **13.** plank nailed to sleepers for stiffening, **14.** lug. *) The next higher values in Table 2 apply to the dimensions of the timbers in this version.

5.1.3 Strengthening by pulling in walls

A wall of bricks or rectangular concrete elements at least 24 cm thick shall be erected between the wall to be reinforced and the opposite wall. Every fourth layer of this masonry must be interlocked with the existing walls. The information contained in Section 5.12 shall apply mutatis mutandis to the foundation of the wall. Door openings should be arranged in the middle of the wall as far as possible and must not be larger than 0.80 x 1.80 m. The door openings must be integrated into the existing walls by interlocking. If there are no steel girders or precast concrete elements for the lintel, a plank at least 6 cm thick shall be laid under the brick lintel.

5.1.4 Vertical wall bracing by wooden constructions

The vertical wall bracing is achieved by wooden frames (see Fig. 3). When manufacturing these frames, the woods that may be required for ceiling bracing should be included in the construction as far as possible. The minimum dimensions of the wooden members and the nails to be used are given in Table 1.

Table 1: Minimum cross-sections of the wooden members for vertical wall bracing

	(m) [1])	Spacing between the bracings in		
	2,40	2,00		1,50
wall timber	14/16	14/14	12/16	12/14
head straps	8/14	8/14	8/12	8/12
threshold	10/14	10/14	10/12	10/12
Single length of the nails [2])	10 cm	10 cm	9 cm	9 cm

1) The distance between the bracings must not be greater than the clear cellar height.
2) The arrangement of the nails is shown in Figure 3.

5.1.5 Reinforcing against radiation exposure

To prevent the penetration of radioactive radiation into the basement, the external walls of basements thinner than 49 cm shall be reinforced as shown in Figures 4 to 6. The protective measures against the penetration of rainwater explained in these figures (upper slope, waterproof foil, water-repellent paint, ballast packing) are necessary to prevent the protective cellar walls from becoming damp.

5.2 Reinforcing ceilings

The ceilings of the protective cellars must meet the requirements set out in Sections 2 and 3. In most cases, bracing will be required to increase the load-bearing capacity of the existing ceilings.

All solid ceilings are suitable as protective ceilings; protective ceilings made of bricks must not be weaker than 11.5 cm. The most suitable stiffening materials are wood, brick and steel. If the ceilings are to be reinforced with precast reinforced concrete elements, experts should be consulted.
Examples of how the bracing of the most frequently occurring types of ceiling can be carried out most expediently are now to be explained.

5.2.1 Cap ceilings

Cap ceilings are arched ceilings made of bricks stretched between steel girders (see Fig. 7). The distance between the girders is usually 1.00 to 1.50 m. The distance between the girders is usually 1.00 to 1.50 m. For these ceilings, the steel girders and caps must be supported as shown in Figures 8 or 9. Direct support of the ceiling girders by masonry pillars must be carried out as shown in Figure 9.

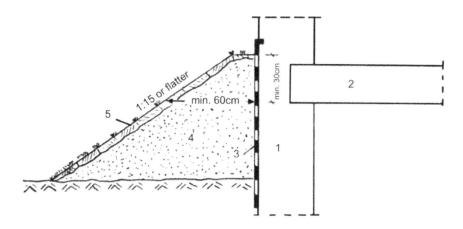

Fig. 4: Radiation protection by earth burial

1. outer wall of the protective cellar, 2. ceiling of the protective cellar, 3. insulation (water-repellent paint, foil, roofing felt or other water-repellent material led down to the existing seal), 4. earth fill, 5. embankment, if possible fasten with grass sods

Fig. 5: Radiation protection by earth filling behind a wooden wall

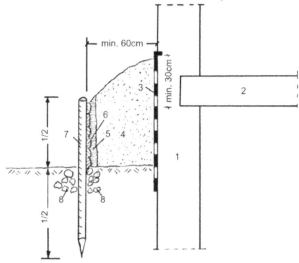

1. external wall of the protective cellar, 2. ceiling of the protective cellar, 3. insulation, 4. earth filling, 5. clay layer, foil or similar. (to prevent the soil from being washed out), 6. boarding (rind boards, sheet metal, etc.), 7. pile (depending on the distance from round timber 8 to 12 cm Ø or squared lumber 10/10 to 16/16), 8. large boulders of stone, etc., to increase the stability of the piles.

The distance between the piles depends on the durability of the boarding. In case of high pile heights, the piles must be driven in with an inclination to the building.

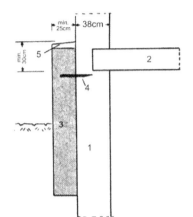

Fig. 6: Radiation protection by facing a wall

1. outer wall of the protective cellar, 2. ceiling of the protective cellar, 3. brick wall (frost-free foundation), 4. round steel (6 to 12 mm Ø and at least 24 cm long, knock firmly into the joints at intervals of approx. 75 cm and then bend by 45°), 5. concrete cover

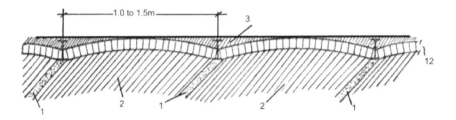

Fig. 7: Cap ceiling

1. steel girder about I 18, 2. brick, 3. concrete

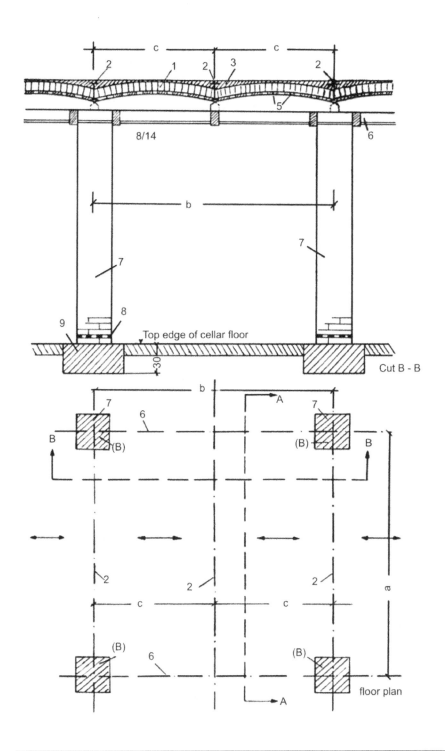

c   c

2   1   2   3   2

5

8/14

6

b

7

7

8

9

Top edge of cellar floor

+30

Cut B - B

b

7   A   7

6

B   (B)   (B)   B

2   2   2

a

c   c

(B)   (B)

6

A

floor plan

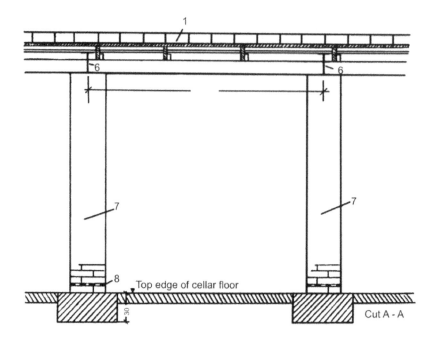

Top edge of cellar floor

Cut A - A

End bearing formation

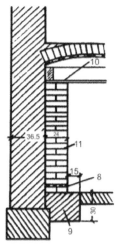

Fig. 8: Support of the cap ceilings by steel joists and supports of masonry

1. cap, 2. cap support, 3. concrete. 4. arch of plank (min. 4 cm thick), 5. economy formwork (3 cm thick), 6. joist (A), 7. pier (B) of bricks and masonry mortar, 8. one layer of cardboard, 9. foundation of concrete or masonry, 10. support length min. equal to the height of the steel girder, 11. pier template (24 x 36,5 cm)

The last four layers of the piers are made of full bricks in cement mortar. Instead, pressure distribution plates made of steel sheet (min. 15 mm), natural stone or prefabricated concrete parts (width min. equal to twice the width of the girder flange) can also be used.

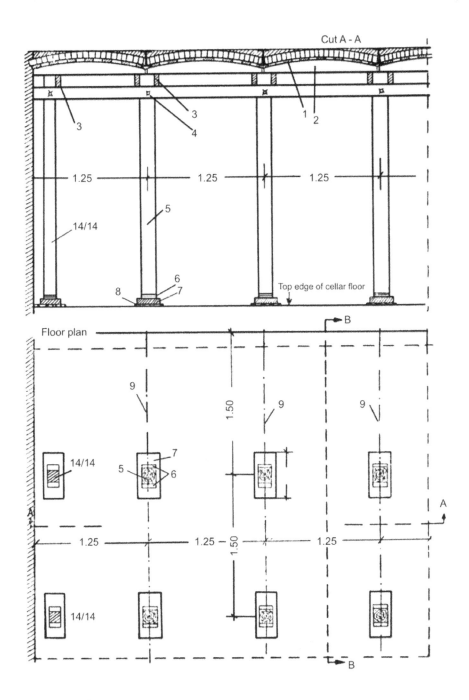

Cut A - A

3
3
4
1
2

1.25   1.25   1.25

14/14

5

6
8   7

Top edge of cellar floor

B

Floor plan

9

1.50

9

9

14/14

7
5   6

A
A

1.25   1.25   1.50   1.25

14/14

B

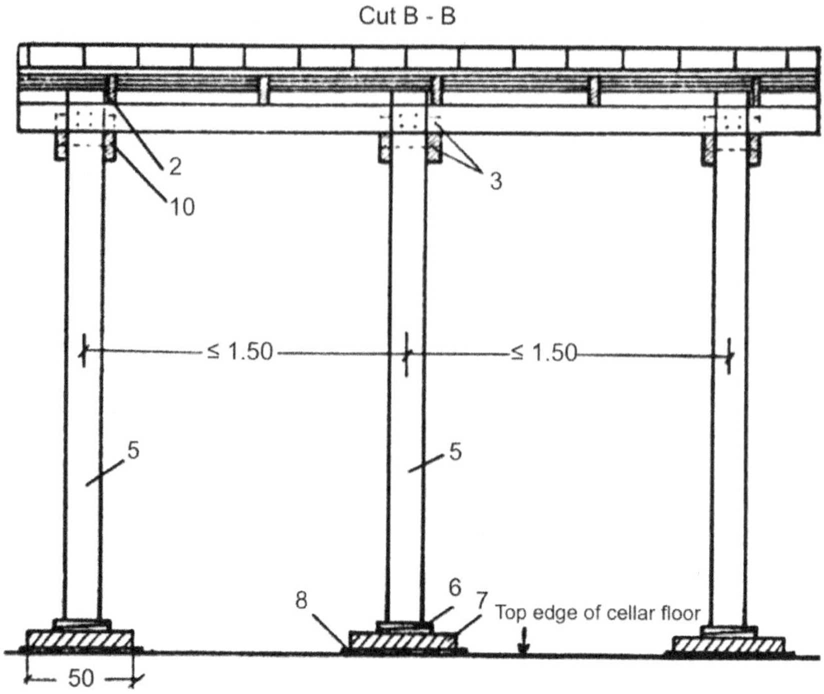

Cut B - B

Fig. 9: Direct support of the ceiling beams of the ceiling cap made of squared lumber or round timber

1. economy formwork (min. 3 cm thick), 2. arch of plank (4 cm thick), 3. pliers 5/12, 4. bolt M 20, 5. support (18 cm Ø or 16/16), 6. wedges, 7. threshold (min. 6 cm thick), 8. one layer of cardboard, 9. support of the cap, 10. 2X4 nails (min. 9 cm long)

Table 2: Direct support of the ceiling girders of the cap ceiling by masonry supports

Distance between ceiling beams	Distance between supports (m)	Minimum dimensions of the supports (cm)
Up to 1.00 m	equal to or smaller than 3.00	24 x 36,5
1.00 m to 1.25 m	equal to or smaller than 2.75	24 x 36,5
1.25 m to 1.50 m	equal to or smaller than 2.50	24 x 36,5

24

5.2.2 Steel block slabs and ribbed reinforced concrete slabs

Steel stone ceilings are stone ceilings reinforced with steel inserts (see Fig. 10). The steels are laid between the perforated bricks and the spaces between them are filled with concrete. A mortar levelling layer is applied over the perforated bricks. Steel block ceilings can be stretched between steel girders or rest on walls. These ceilings are to be shuttered and reinforced as shown in Figure 11. Reinforced concrete ribbed slabs shall be braced in the same manner.

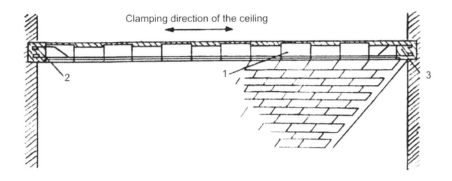

Fig. 10: Steel stone ceiling

1. perforated brick, 2. steel inlays, 3. solid concrete strips

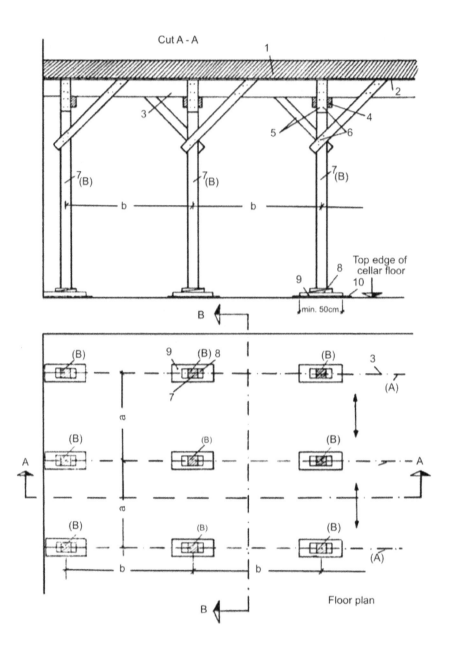

Cut A - A

7(B)   7(B)   7(B)

b   b

Top edge of
cellar floor

8
9   10

min. 50cm

B

(B)   9 (B) 8   (B)   3

7   (A)

a

A   (B)   (B)   (B)   A

a

(B)   (B)   (B)

(A)

b   b

B

Floor plan

26

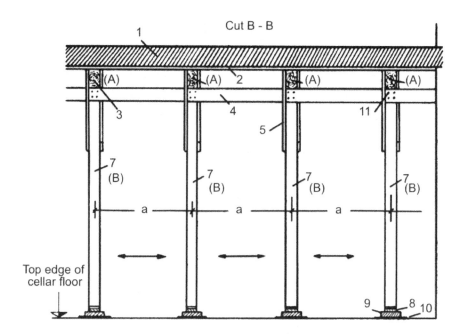

Fig. 11: Support of the steel stone slabs by beams and supports made of squared lumber or round timber

1. ceiling, 2. cladding (min. 2.4 cm thick), 3. beam (A), 4. pliers 5/12, 5. board flaps (min. 2.4 cm thick), 6. 2 x 4 nails each (min. 9 cm long), 7. prop (B). 8. wedges, 9. threshold (min. 6 cm thick). 10. one layer of cardboard, 11. 4 nails (10 cm long)

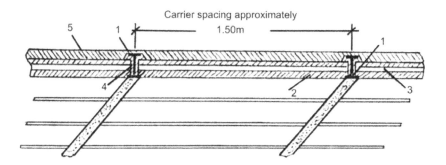

Fig. 12: Hollow reinforced concrete planks

1. steel girders, 2. hollow reinforced concrete planks, 3. cavities, 4. cement mortar, 5. flooring

5.2.3 Hollow reinforced concrete floorboards

Hollow reinforced concrete floorboards are reinforced concrete slabs with cavities in their longitudinal direction (see Fig. 12). They are generally laid on the lower flanges of steel girders or on masonry. The spacing of the steel girders is up to 1.50 m. If the hollow planks rest on walls, their span can be up to 2.50 m. The distance between the steel girders is up to 1.50 m. The thickness of the hollow planks varies between 6 and 12 cm, the planks are 25 or 33 cm wide. Hollow planks between steel girders are supported as shown in Figure 13. The dimensions are given in Table 3.

Table 3: Reinforced concrete hollow plank slab between steel girders supported by beams (A) and columns (B) of squared lumber or round timber

Prop spacing	Beams (A) Minimum dimensions (cm)	Prop (B) Minimum dimensions (cm)
Up to 1.50 m	12/14 Ø 16	Ø 12 10/12
1.50 m to 2.00 m	14/18 16/16 Ø 19	Ø 14 12/14
2.00 m to 2,50 m	12/24 14/22 16/20 Ø 22	Ø 16 14/14 12/16

If the span of the planks when supported on walls is greater than 1.20 m, the bracing must be carried out as shown in Figure 11, whereby the underside of the ceiling is not covered.

5.2.4 Reinforced concrete ceilings

Reinforced concrete ceilings are concrete ceilings with steel inserts (see Fig. 14). The following bracing options refer only to reinforced concrete ceilings with a flat underside. They must be braced as shown in Figure 11 (but without the cladding of the underside).

5.2.5 Stone ceilings between steel girders

These are flat slabs of perforated bricks stretched between steel girders (see Fig. 15). The height of the perforated bricks is 10 to 15 cm. These ceilings are to be shuttered and braced according to Figures 16 and 17. If possible, no protective cellars should be set up under unreinforced stone ceilings. If it is necessary in exceptional cases, this ceiling can be approved for distances of up to 1.00 m between beams.

Cut A - A

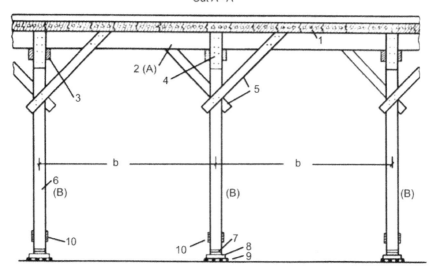

Floor plan

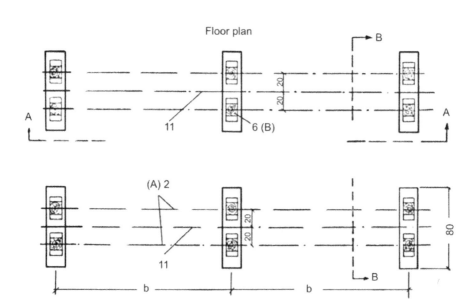

Cut B - B

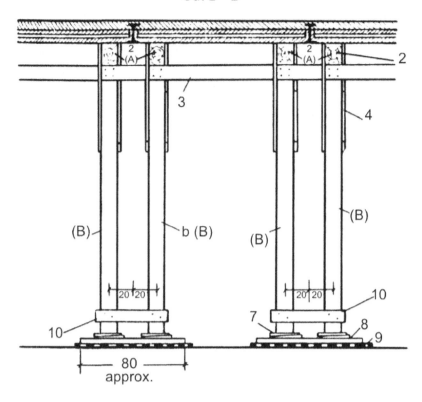

Fig. 13: Support of hollow reinforced concrete planks between steel girders

1. hollow reinforced concrete planks, 2. beam (A), 3. pliers (5/12 cm), 4. tabs (2.4 cm thick)
2 x 4 nails min. 9 cm long, 5. tabs (min. 2.4 cm thick) 2 x 4 nails min. 9 cm long, 6. support (B), 7. wedges, 8. threshold (min. 6 cm thick), 9. one layer of cardboard, 10. board flap (min. 2.4 cm thick) 2X2 nails min. 9 cm long, 11. ceiling girde

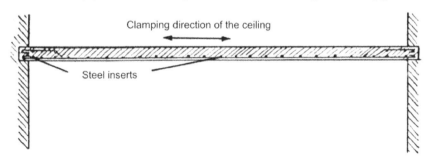

Fig. 14: Reinforced concrete ceiling with flat ceiling underside

31

Cut A - A

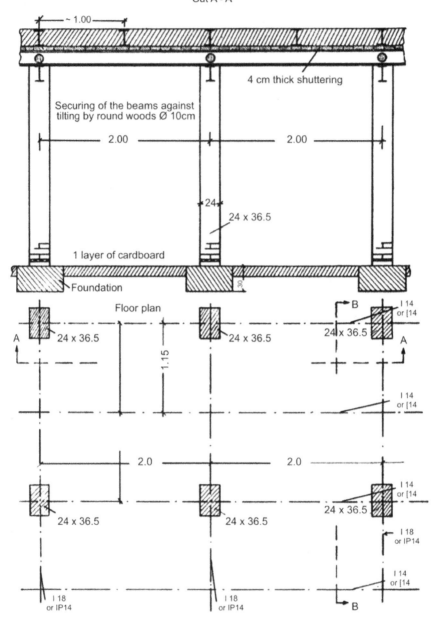

~ 1.00

4 cm thick shuttering

Securing of the beams against
tilting by round woods Ø 10cm

2.00   2.00

24

24 x 36.5

1 layer of cardboard

Foundation

30

Floor plan

B

I 14
or [14

A   24 x 36.5   24 x 36.5   24 x 36.5   A

1.15

I 14
or [14

2.0   2.0

I 14
or [14

24 x 36.5   24 x 36.5   24 x 36.5

I 18
or IP14

I 14
or [14

I 18
or IP14   I 18
or IP14   B

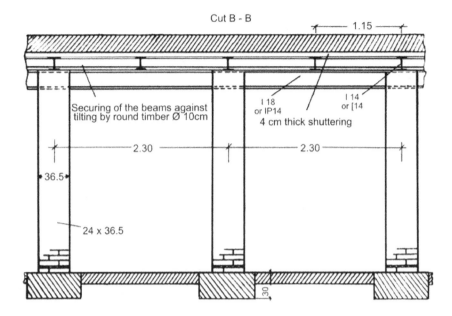

Cut B - B

1.15

Securing of the beams against
tilting by round timber Ø 10cm

I 18
or IP14

I 14
or [14

4 cm thick shuttering

2.30

2.30

36.5

24 x 36.5

30

Fig. 16: Support of stone slabs by steel beams and masonry columns and mortar

The last seven layers of the piers are made of bricks and cement mortar. Instead,
pressure distribution plates made of steel sheet (min. 15 mm), natural stone or
prefabricated concrete parts (width min. equal to twice the width of the girder
flange) can also be used.

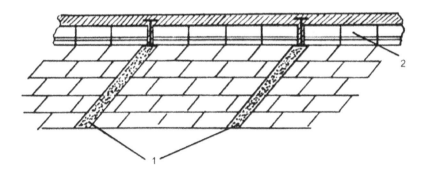

2

1

Fig. 15: Stone ceiling between steel beams

1. steel beam, 2. perforated brick

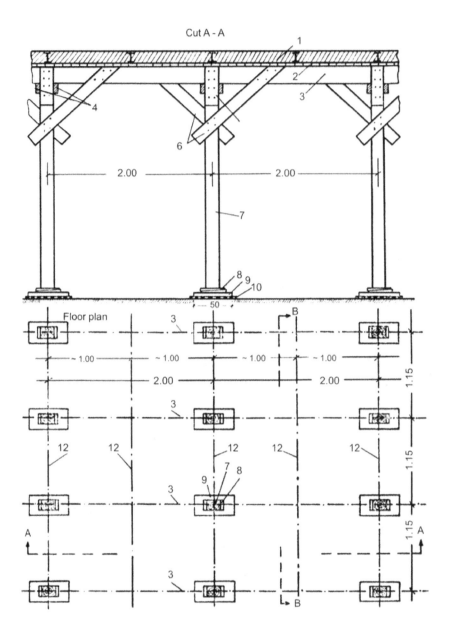

Cut A - A

Floor plan

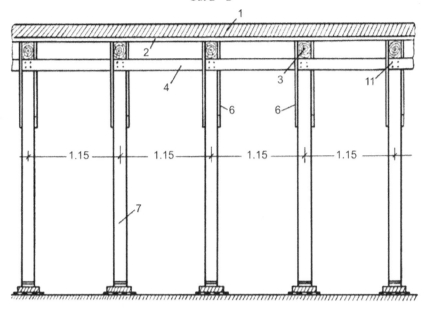

Cut B - B

Fig. 17: Support of stone slabs by beams and supports made of squared lumber or round timber

1. ceiling, 2. cladding (min. 4 cm thick), 3. beam 14/20, 18/18, 12/22 or Ø 22, 4. pliers 5/12, 5. flap (2 x 4 nails min. 9 cm long), 6. board flaps min. 2.4 cm thick (2 x 4 nails min. 9 cm long), 7. support 14/16 or Ø 17, 8. wedges, 9. threshold (min. 6 cm thick), 10. one layer of cardboard, 11. 4 nails 10 cm, 12. ceiling girder

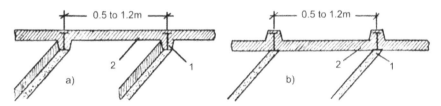

Fig. 18: Unreinforced concrete slabs between steel girders

Version a and b: 1. steel girder, 2. unreinforced concrete

5.2.6 Unreinforced concrete ceilings between steel girders

The concrete ceilings are tensioned horizontally between steel girders (see Fig. 18). The distance between the girders is generally 0.50 to 1.20 m. The construction of the bracing corresponds to that of the stone slabs between steel girders (see section 5.25).

5.2.7 Hollow body ceilings

Hollow body ceilings consist of precast reinforced concrete elements (beams) and fillers (see Fig. 19). The fillers are suspended between the beams and the gussets are concreted out.
These hollow body ceilings are to be supported and shuttered as shown in Figure 20.

5.2.8 Zwickau ceilings

The Zwickau ceilings are ceilings made of precast reinforced concrete elements (see Fig. 21). They consist of individual ceiling elements that span the room. In order to obtain a smooth underside of the ceiling, lightweight panels are attached to the undersides of the elements, which are then plastered.
The Zwickau ceiling should be braced in the same way as the hollow body ceiling, whereby the filler wood under the concrete beams is omitted (see Fig. 20).

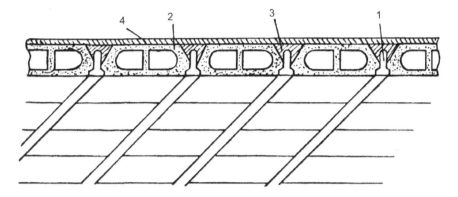

Fig. 19: Hollow body ceiling

1. beam, 2. filler, 3. concrete, 4. floor

5.2.9 Instructions for execution

Beams made of squared lumber must always be installed on edge. If no squared lumber is available in the required length, it must be pushed over a support as shown in Figure 22. If possible, the width and height of the saddle timber should be the same as that of the joist. At least 2.4 cm thick and 10 cm wide boards are to be used as board flaps.
When wedging the supports, care must be taken that the wedges are not tightened too much so that the ceiling is not lifted. The foundation of the wall pillars can be carried out as shown in Figure 23.

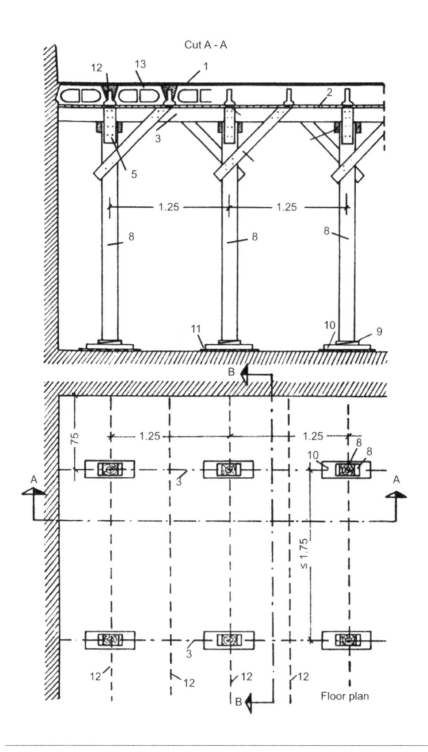

Cut A - A

Floor plan

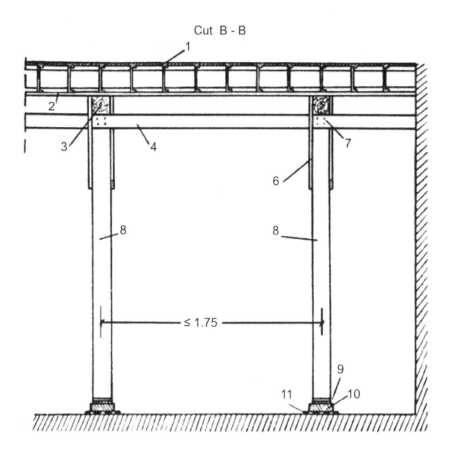

Cut B - B

Fig. 20: Support of DIN-F ceilings by beams and supports made of squared lumber or round timber

1. hollow body ceiling, 2. shuttering (min. 3 cm thick), 3. beam (min. 14/14 or Ø 17), 4. pliers 5/12, 5. board plates (both sides) each with 2 x 4 nails (min. 2 x 4 nails) 9 cm long), 6. board tabs (min. 2.4 cm thick) each with 2X nails (min. 9 cm long), 7. 4 nails (min. 10 cm long), 8. support (min. 14/16 or Ø 17), 9. wedges. 10. threshold (6 cm thick), 11. one layer of plywood board, 12. DIN-F beam, 13. filler, 14. filling wood (min. 5 cm thick)

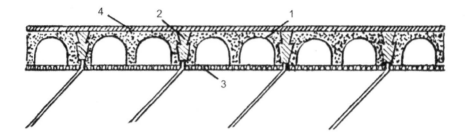

Fig. 21: Zwickau ceiling

1. ceiling elements, 2. concrete, 3. lightweight boards, 4. flooring

5.3 Entrance

5.3.1 Arrangement of the entrance

The entrance, which in any case must be equipped with a sluice, is located in a well-protected place in the basement. The sluice is closed to the outside by a gas-tight pressure door and to the inside, to the lounge, by a gas-tight door. The sluice must be able to accommodate at least two persons at the same time (see Figs. 24 and 25). In front of the outer door, the ceiling of the cellar corridor must be braced in full width and in a length corresponding to twice the corridor width (see section 5.2).
A container with chlorinated lime is placed in front of the gas-tight pressure door in the cellar corridor.

5.3.2 Sluice

5.3.2.1 Sluice in cellar corridor

The position of the sluice in the cellar corridor must be chosen so that there are as few openings as possible to other cellar rooms (see Fig. 24). Unused openings must be closed gas-tight, pressure- and radiation-proof. Cleaning openings of chimneys must be sealed, as explained in Section 5.6.

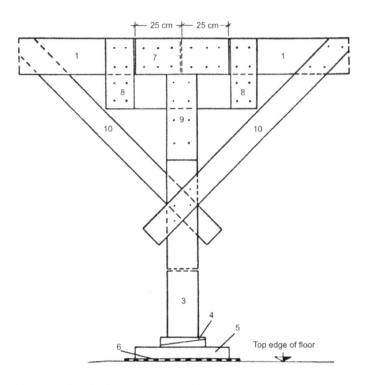

Fig. 22: Attaching the plank lugs when the joist is butted with saddle timber and support

1. beam, 2. saddle timber (70 cm long), 3. prop, 4. wedges, 5. threshold, 6. one layer of plywood, 7. board tab (12 nails), 8. board tab (8 nails), 9. board tab (8 nails), 10. board tab (8 nails).
Thickness of the board tabs 2.4 cm, nail length min. 9 cm.
The plank tabs 7, 8 and 9 are to be attached in the same way to the side of the joist or saddle timber and the prop facing away from the observer.

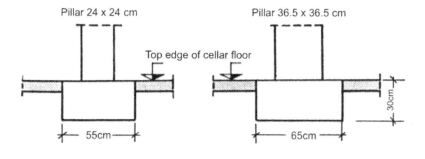

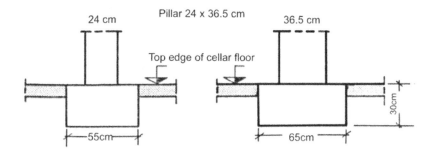

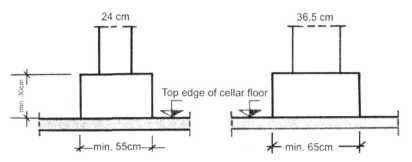

Fig. 23: Formation of the pier foundations

a) Foundations under top edge of basement floor (masonry or concrete)
b) Foundations above upper edge of basement floor (brickwork finish)
Foundations above the basement floor can possibly be used as seating. They must then be built higher and wider.

5.3.2.2 Sluice in the common room

The sluice in the common room is designed as a porch-like installation (see Fig. 25). Its walls can be made of full-groove masonry (at least 11.5 cm thick) with smooth joint coating or of wood covered with paper. Particular attention must be paid to a gas-tight connection between the lock walls and the ceiling and floor of the recreation room.

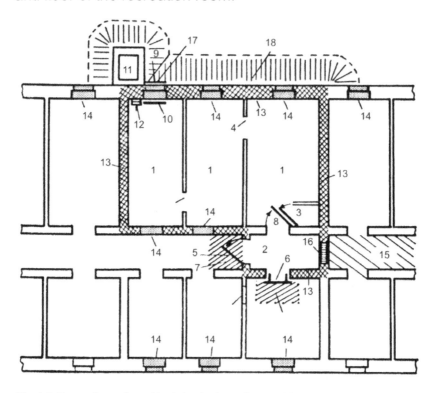

Fig. 24: Protective cellar with sluice in the cellar corridor

1. lounge, 2. sluice, 3. dry toilet, 4. wall opening in existing wall, 5. gas-tight pressure door, 6. gas- and pressure-proof closure (emergency solution if cut-off basement room cannot be made accessible from adjacent room through wall opening (17)), 7. ceiling bracing to protect the gas-tight pressure door (5) and the gas- and pressure-proof closure (6), 8. gas-tight door, 9. gas-tight pressure flap, 10. gas-tight flap, 11. coarse sand filter, 12. bellows fan, 13. enclosure walls of the protective cellar, 14. pressure- and radiation-proof closed doors and windows, 15. connecting corridor to the neighbouring protective cellar, 16. bricked up opening in the fire wall, 17. emergency exit (through cellar window), 18. earth fill as radiation protection

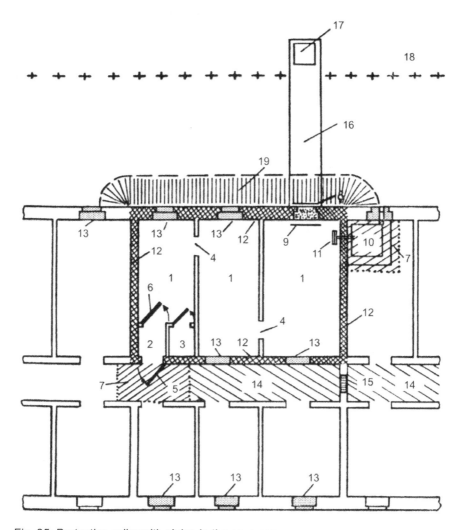

Fig. 25: Protective cellar with sluice in the common room

1. lounge, 2. sluice, 3. dry toilet, 4. wall opening in existing wall, 5. gastight pressure door, 6. gastight door, 7. ceiling bracing to protect the gastight pressure door and the coarse sand filter, 8. gastight pressure flap, 9. gastight flap, 10. coarse sand filter, 11. bellows fan, 12. Enclosure walls of the protective cellar, 13. pressure- and radiation-proof closed doors and windows, 14. connecting corridor to the neighbouring protective cellar, 15. walled breakthrough in the fire wall, 16. emergency outlet, 17. emergency exit, 18. boundary of the rubble area, 19. earth fill as radiation protection

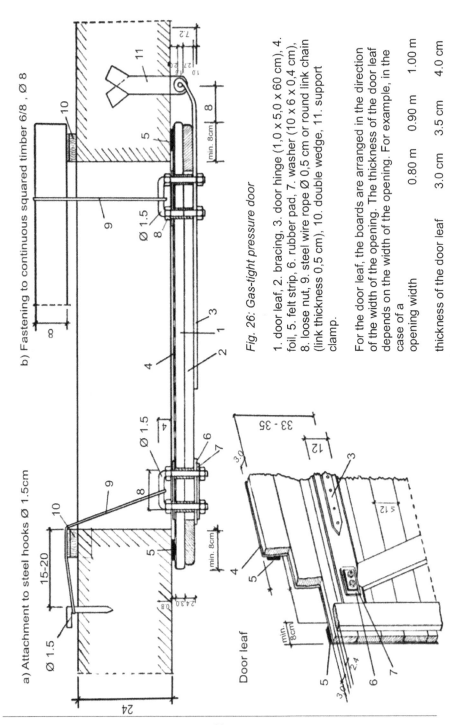

b) Fastening to continuous squared timber 6/8 , Ø 8

a) Attachment to steel hooks Ø 1.5cm

Door leaf

Fig. 26: Gas-tight pressure door

1. door leaf, 2. bracing, 3. door hinge (1,0 x 5,0 x 60 cm), 4. foil, 5. felt strip, 6. rubber pad, 7. washer (10 x 6 x 0,4 cm), 8. loose nut, 9. steel wire rope Ø 0,5 cm or round link chain (link thickness 0,5 cm), 10. double wedge, 11. support clamp.

For the door leaf, the boards are arranged in the direction of the width of the opening. The thickness of the door leaf depends on the width of the opening. For example, in the case of a

opening width	0.80 m	0.90 m	1.00 m
thickness of the door leaf	3.0 cm	3.5 cm	4.0 cm

46

5.3.3 Doors

5.3.3.1 Gas-tight wooden pressure doors

The gas-tight pressure door shall have a clear height of not more than 1.80 m and a clear width of not more than 0.80 m. The gas-tight pressure door shall have a clear height of not more than 1.80 m and a clear width of not more than 0.80 m. The door leaf strikes from the outside (see Figs. 24 and 25) and has a minimum 8 cm stop on all sides. It is advisable to design the gas-tight pressure door as a board door, as shown in Figure 26. The thickness of the door leaf depends on the width of the door opening.

Door opening width:	0.80 m	0.90 m	1.0 m
Thickness of door leaf	3.0 cm	3.5 cm	4.0 cm

If an existing cellar door is used as a gastight pressure door (see Fig. 27), it must be reinforced with the following board thicknesses, depending on the width of the door opening:

Door opening width:	0.80 m	0.90 m	1.0 m
Thickness of the additional Reinforcement:	$\geqq$2.6 cm	3.0 cm	3.5 cm

If brickwork is present on all sides for the door stop, a smooth strip of mortar (mortar group II) is plastered in the area of the stop in order to obtain a flat surface for the door edge seal. If there is no masonry stop at the top or bottom edge of the door, it can be made by squared lumber 10/12 or 10/10. The squared lumber is placed on one level with the plaster strip and is walled in on both sides of the door opening. Door thresholds must not be higher than 10 cm.

Felt strips 5 to 8 mm thick and 4 cm wide are used as a seal between the door leaf and the plaster edge, which must be carefully fastened to the door leaf. Hose profiles with an outer diameter of approx. 15 mm and a wall thickness of approx. 2 mm are also suitable for this purpose. They must be fixed in a groove 12 mm deep and 9 mm wide, formed by two strips nailed to the door leaf. Hose profiles should only be cut diagonally at the corners of the door leaves.

By gluing foils, multi-layered paper or by applying wood fibre boards, plywood or similar to the inside of the door, it is ensured that it is gas-tight.
The door hinges are arranged at a distance of 0.35 m from the upper or lower edge of the door leaf. The pivot point of the hinges must be positioned so that it is a small distance from the wall, but a larger distance from the door leaf.

Simple closures are shown in Figure 26. If locking levers are used, one must be fitted at the level of each door hinge. They must be attached to the cams from below so that the lock is not unintentionally opened by debris which may fall on the end of the lever.
All anchors must be 20 cm in length.

Cut through the gas-tight pressure door

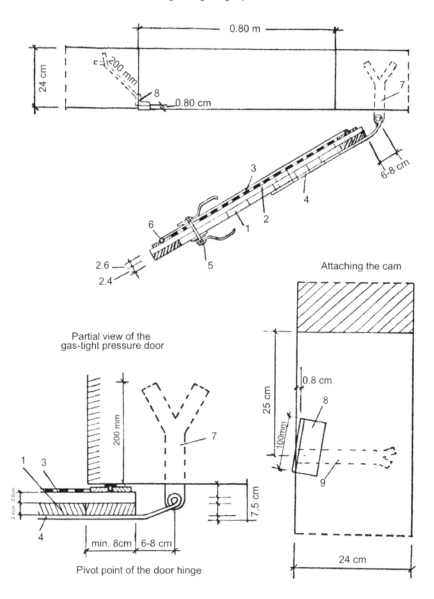

Partial view of the
gas-tight pressure door

Attaching the cam

Pivot point of the door hinge

Reinforced cellar door

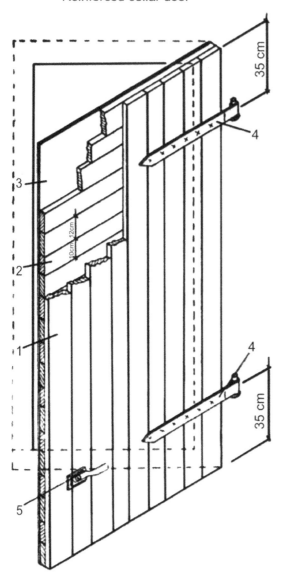

Fig. 27: Reinforced cellar door as gastight pressure door

The reinforcement of the existing cellar door depends on the width of the opening (see section 5.331). The door leaf covers the opening on all sides by at least 8 cm.

1. the door leaf of the existing cellar door,
2. reinforcement (2.6 cm thick), 3. foil multilayer paper, wood fibre boards or similar,
4. door hinge, 5. lock, 6. rubber hose Ø 15 mm, 7. support clamp (50 x 10 mm), 8. angle steel cam (50 x 50 x 6 mm), 9. welded anchor

5.3.3.2 Gas-tight wooden doors

The gas-tight door strikes from the inside. The width of the stop is 6 cm. Figure 28 shows an example of the design. A 2.4 cm thick door leaf is sufficient for the gas-tight door. Longitudinal and diagonal bracing must be arranged on the side of the sluice. All anchors must be inserted at least 12 cm into the masonry. For the gaskets and the installation of the door hinges, the versions under 5.331 apply.
The door locks can be designed as shown in Figures 28, 29 and 41.

5.3.3.3 Steel doors

In the case of steel doors, it is usually only possible to use existing doors. If a steel door is to be used as a gas-tight pressure door, it must be statically proven whether it is suitable for this purpose. Any steel door that is not damaged can be used as a gas-tight door. The doors must be sealed in accordance with the requirements for wooden doors. Installation in the wall opening must be carried out with a frame made of angle steel (at least 40 x 80 x 6 mm). The leg thickness must not be less than 6 mm. The longer side of the leg must be used as a stop.

The steel frames must be fastened with welded anchors (see Fig. 30). The same requirements apply to the length of the anchors as for wooden doors. At door height, at least three anchors must be provided on each side, and at least one in the transverse direction of the frame, top and bottom. Make sure that there is a good seal between the frame and the brickwork.

5.4 Connecting passages

If there are several protective cellars in a block of flats, these must be connected with each other by rubble-proof corridors (see Fig. 31). These corridors must be braced in accordance with section 5.2, but the cladding may be omitted. Necessary openings in fire walls shall be made as shown in Figure 32. These openings shall be closed as shown in this figure, using clay mortar.

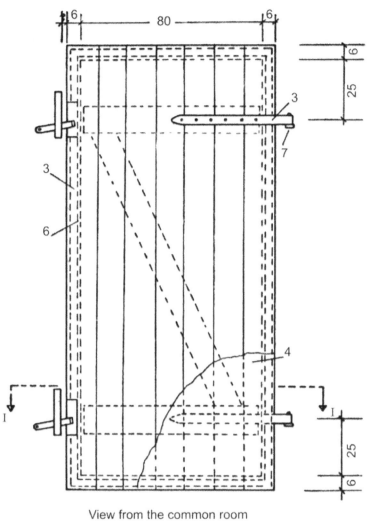

View from the common room

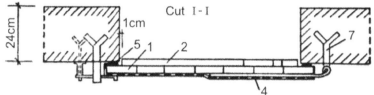

Cut I - I

Clasp

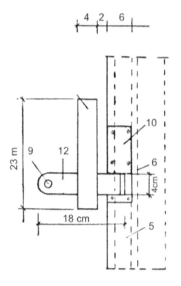

View from the common room

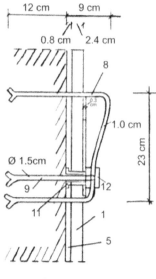

Side view

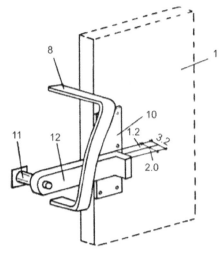

Fig. 28: Gas-tight door

1. door leaf (2.4 cm thick), 2. bracing, 3. door hinge, 4. foil, cardboard or multi-ply paper glued on, 5. felt strips (0.5-0.8 cm thick, 3-4 cm wide), 6. boundary of door opening, 7. support clamp, 8. Bracket as anchor 12 cm in masonry, 9. joint (Ø 1.5 cm) 12 cm long as anchor in masonry, 10. sheet metal (0.3 x 6.0 x 15.0 cm) screwed on, 11. spacer (Ø 2 cm) welded onto plate 4 x 4 cm between sash fastener and masonry, 12. sash fastener

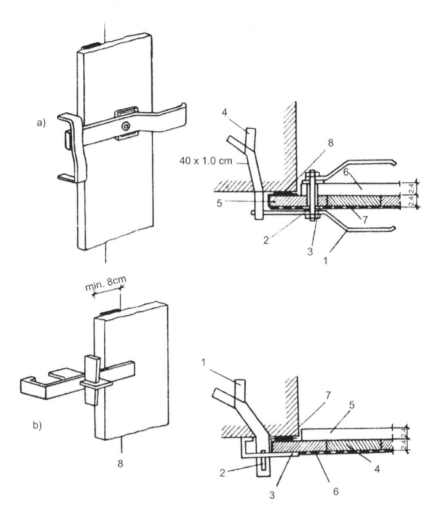

Fig. 29: Closing possibilities of the gas-tight door

On the gas-tight door, two latches are to be arranged at the same height as the door hinges.

a) Lever lock: 1. lever, 2. washer, 3. rubber pad, 4. bracket as anchor 12 cm in masonry, 5. door leaf (2.4 cm thick), 6. stiffening of door leaf (2.4 cm thick), 7. foil, 8. felt strips
b) wedged lock: 1. steel strip (1 cm thick) as anchor 12 cm in masonry, 2. wedge, 3. steel strip (1 cm thick), 4. door leaf (2.4 cm thick), 5. stiffening of door leaf, 6. foil, paper or similar glued on, 7. felt strip This lock is not fastened to door leaf

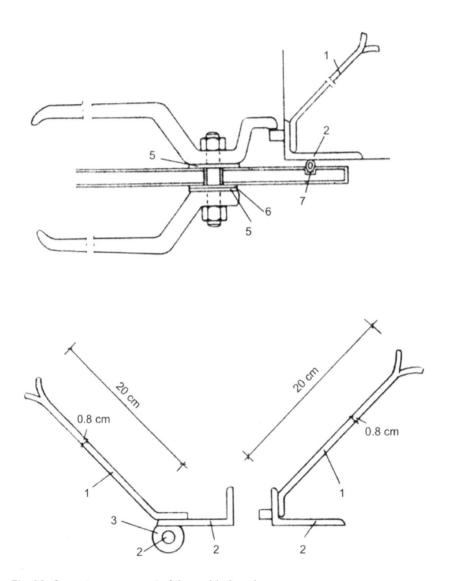

Fig. 30: Correct arrangement of the welded anchors

1. anchor (0.8 cm), 2. angle profile (4.0 x 8.0 x 0.6 cm), 3. support clamp, 4. bore (clear width 1.5 cm), 5. washer, 6. rubber pad, 7. gasket

5.5 Emergency exits

5.5.1 Emergency exits outside the debris area

In the case of individual protective cellars, an emergency outlet must generally be installed which ends outside the debris area. If several basements are connected by corridors, at least two emergency exits must be provided outside the debris area if more than 200 persons are to be accommodated in the basements. The location of emergency exits shall be determined in accordance with local conditions. Emergency exits may be made in accordance with Figures 33, 34 and 35. The size of the debris area is shown in Figure 36.

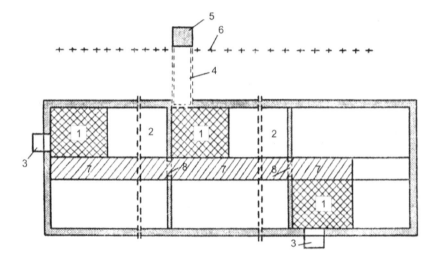

Fig. 31: Example of the arrangement of emergency exits and connecting corridors

1. day room, 2. distance between the day rooms (min. 30 m), 3. emergency exit at the outer wall of the building, 4. creeper of the emergency outlet, 5. emergency exit of the emergency outlet outside the rubble area, 6. border of the rubble area, 7. rubble-proof connecting passage, 8. breakthrough in fire wall

5.5.2 Emergency exits on the outside wall of the building

Protective cellars connected by corridors, which do not have their own emergency exit outside the rubble area, are given an emergency exit on the outer wall of the building (see Fig. 31). Cellar windows with openings of at least 0.60 x 0.60 m are suitable for this purpose. The emergency exits are prepared according to Figs. 37 or 38.

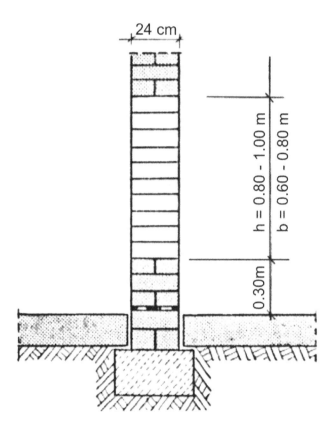

Fig. 32: Breakthrough through a fire wall

The opening in the fire wall is bricked and grouted with bricks in clay mortar without a special bond.

Light shafts can also be used as exit shafts. Emergency exit openings must be filled with earth. If the cellar ceiling is above the top edge of the ground, a ground fill (see Fig. 39) or dry brickwork is recommended as wall reinforcement for the emergency exit (see also Section 5.15).

5.6 Closing of openings

All openings that are not required must be closed gas-tight, pressure- and radiation-proof. Door and window openings in the enclosing walls of protective cellars are bricked up with full-joint brickwork to the full thickness of the wall. Window openings can also be closed as shown in Figure 40. The window and door openings of rooms adjoining or facing a protective cellar shall be closed in a radiation and splinter-proof manner.

If a door opening to be closed is the only access to a used adjacent cellar room, it shall be sealed in accordance with Figure 41 so that the cellar is not out of use for a longer period of time.

If chimney cleaning openings are located in a protective cellar, the chimney cavities must be filled with sand up to the upper edge of the protective ceiling.

6 Technical equipment

6.1 Ventilation

Fresh air is supplied via coarse sand filters, which must be located outside the protective cellar. To suck in the air, manually operated bellows fans are used. Figures 24 and 25 show how the ventilation system is to be arranged. If the filter has to be installed in the cellar as an exception, the upper part of the ceiling must be reinforced (see Fig. 25).
The basic structure of the coarse sand filter is shown in Figure 42, while Figures 43 to 47 show examples of the filter design. Concrete or steel pipes can be used for the round filter bodies.

The coarse sand fill in the filter must be 1.00 m high. In the case of rectangular filter cross-sections, shapes as close as possible to the square should be used. If tubes are used as filter bodies, larger diameters should always be preferred. If more than two tubes are used, they are arranged in two rows. The coarse sand fill must consist of clean, as dry as possible, sharp-edged sand with grain dimensions of 0.5 mm to 5 mm and must be filled loosely. This sand should correspond approximately to a good, sieved, sharp-edged wall or concrete sand. Gravel, chippings or gravel with grain sizes of 15 to 30 mm should be used for the base layer.

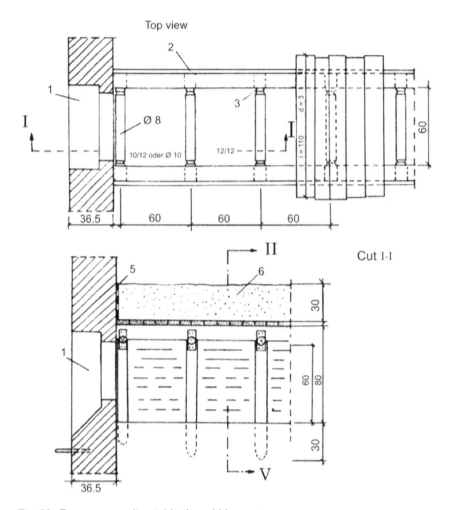

Fig. 33: Emergency exit outside the rubble area

The emergency exit outside the rubble area is connected to the protective cellar by the crawling gear. A window opening of the protective cellar is to be used as access to the crawl passage, which can be sealed as shown in Figures 37, 38 and 40. The crawl passage is closed horizontally at the top with planks (3 cm thick) and covered with a 30 cm thick layer of earth. The sections I-I and II-II show details of the crawling gait.
The structure of the emergency exit can be seen in the sections III-III and IV-IV. Its clear width is 60 x 50 cm. The cover of the emergency exit is released from the inside, falls down and releases the exit opening. The 30 cm thick layer of earth applied as a cover accommodates the approx. 30 cm deep excavation.

1. window opening (62,5 x 50,0 cm), 2. boards (3,0 cm thick), 3. flap, 4. squared lumber 10/12, 5. plywood, 6. filled earth

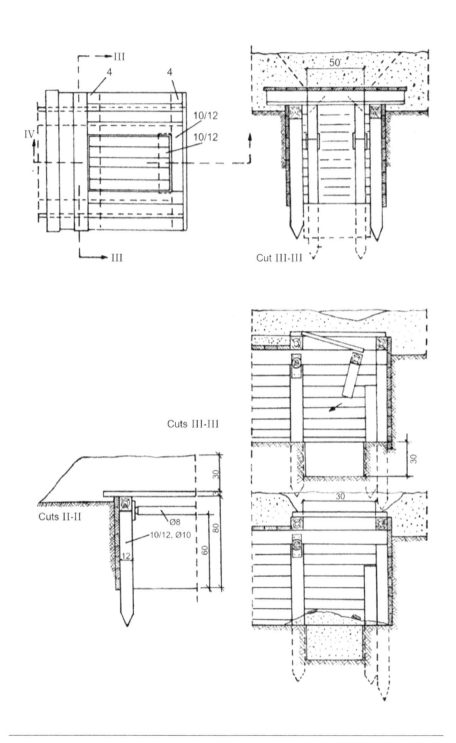

III

4   4

10/12

10/12

IV

III

Cut III-III

50

Cuts III-III

Cuts II-II

Ø8

10/12, Ø10

12

30

3

80

60

30

30

Top View

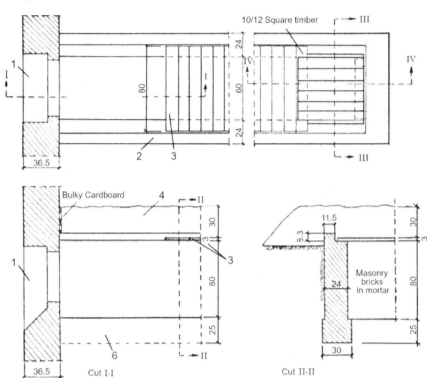

10/12 Square timber

Bulky Cardboard

Masonry bricks in mortar

Cut I-I

Cut II-II

Cut III-III

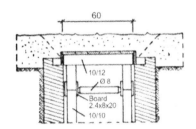

10/12
Ø 8
Board 2.4x8x20
10/10

Cut IV-IV

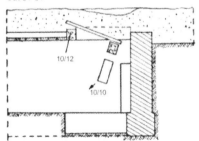

10/12
10/10

Cut IV-IV

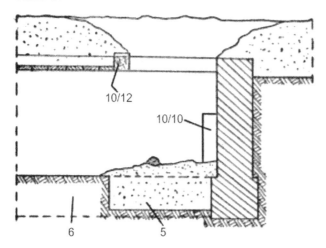

Fig. 34: Emergency exit outside the rubble area

The emergency exit outside the rubble area is connected to the protective cellar by the crawling gear. A window opening of the protective cellar (1) is to be used as access to the crawl passage, which can be sealed according to Figures 37, 38 and 40. The enclosure of the creeper passage (2) consists of brickwork (bricks and mortar, 24 cm thick). The creep passage is closed off horizontally at the top with boards (3 cm thick) or prefabricated parts (3) and covered with a 30 cm thick layer of earth (4). Bulk board (7) protects the masonry from moisture. Sections I-I and II-II show details of the creep speed.

The structure of the emergency exit is shown in sections III-III and IV-IV. Its clear width is 60 x 60 cm. Earth is to be poured on the emergency exit only shortly before the use of the common room. The cover of the emergency exit is loosened from the inside, falls down and opens the exit opening. The recess (5) in the foundation (6) of the emergency exit accommodates the falling earth.

Gratings can be made of bricks or hollow bricks. Steel gratings (light well covers etc.) or slatted gratings are also suitable (see Figs. 45 and 48).

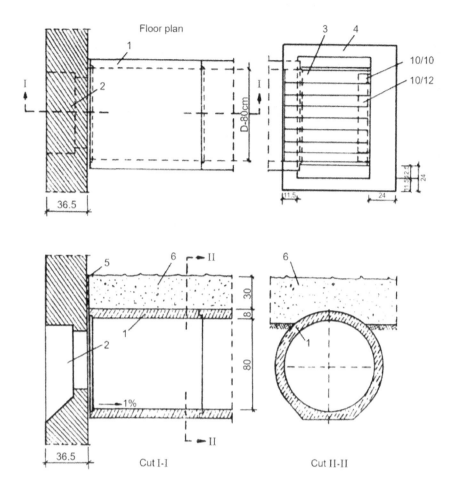

Fig. 35: Emergency exit outside the rubble area

Concrete pipes with a diameter of 80 cm are used for the creep speed. A window opening is used as access from the protective cellar to the creep passage, which can be sealed according to Figures 37, 38 and 40. Details of the emergency exit can be found in Figure 34. The creeper and emergency exit are covered with a 30 cm thick layer of earth.

1. concrete pipe (Ø 80 cm), 2. window opening, 3. covering boards (3 cm thick). 4. masonry, 5. cardboard, 6. filled earth

The filter body must be gas-tight from the upper edge of the coarse sand bed so that no "wrong" air is sucked in. The air sampling openings must be located as far as possible from the supply air pipe so that the air flows through the entire filter cross-section (see Fig. 42).
The bellows fan can be designed and mounted as shown in Figure 49. The required dimensions are shown in the table for Figure 50.

6.2 Lighting, electrical energy supply

The energy for lighting the basement and its access routes shall be drawn from the public grid. If possible, an independent circuit in a damp room design should be laid from the house connection to the protective cellar. The fuse protection must be arranged in the protective cellar. It is recommended to create connection possibilities for radiators, hotplates, immersion heaters and radio receivers in the common rooms.

Battery lights (torches, battery lamps) should be provided in the basement as emergency lighting. Lighting equipment with an open flame (candles, lanterns) should only be used in an emergency and as close as possible to the airlock.
If luminous paint or another light color is present, protruding corners, doors, thresholds, etc. must be marked with it in the protective cellar and in the connecting corridors.

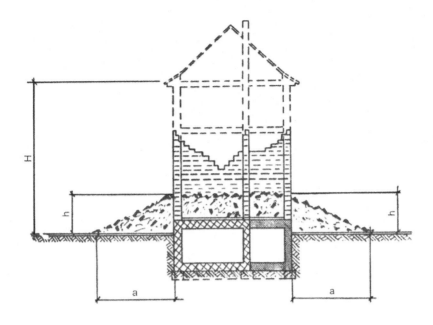

Fig. 36: Size of the debris area

Construction method	a	h
Brick structures H $\leqq$ 30 m	½ H	¼ H
Brick structures H < 30 m	15 m	¼ H
infilled reinforced concrete or steel skeleton structures	¼ H	1/8 H

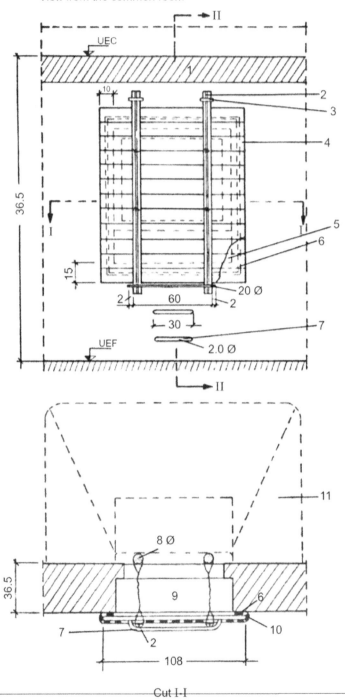

View from the common room

Cut I-I

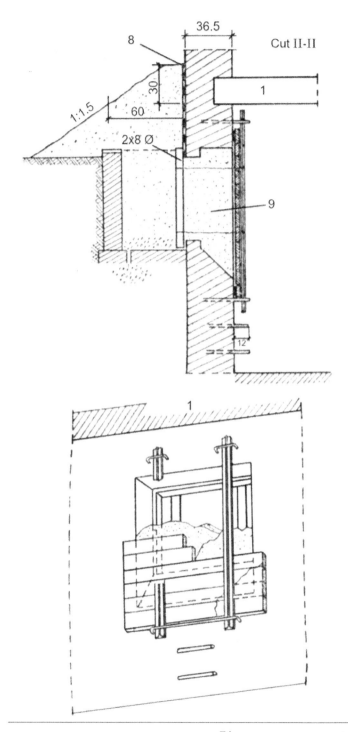

Cut II-II

Fig. 37: Emergency exit on the outside wall of the building

1. ceiling, 2. profile (6 x 3 cm), 3. bracket as anchor 12 cm in masonry, 4. boards (d = 30 cm, b = ≦ 12 cm), 5. surface sealing by glued-on foil or similar, 6. edge sealing by felt strips (d = 5-8 mm, b = 3 cm) on level, plastered surface, 7. crampons, 8. cardboard, 9. sand filling in the window opening, 10. foil is led around up to the felt strip, 11. earth filling

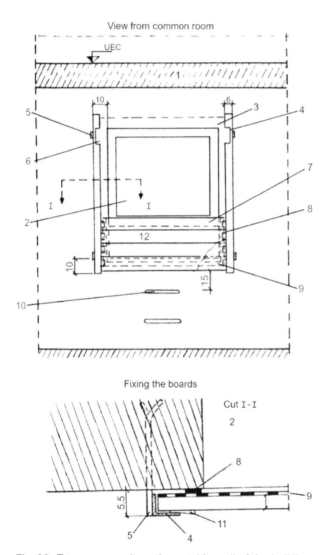

Fig. 38: Emergency exit on the outside wall of the building

1. ceiling, 2. window opening (min. 50 x 60 cm) with sand filling, 3. flat, plastered surface, 4. angle profile (40 x 60 x 5 mm), 5. anchor (10 x 40 mm) 12 cm in masonry, 6. opening for plank insertion, 7. inserted and wedged boards (d = 3 cm), 8. edge seal by felt strips (d = 5-8 mm, b = 3 cm), 9. surface seal by glued-on foil or similar, 10. crampons (if greater height is to be overcome), 11. wedge
Before the window is opened, a ground fill is carried out (see Fig. 37).

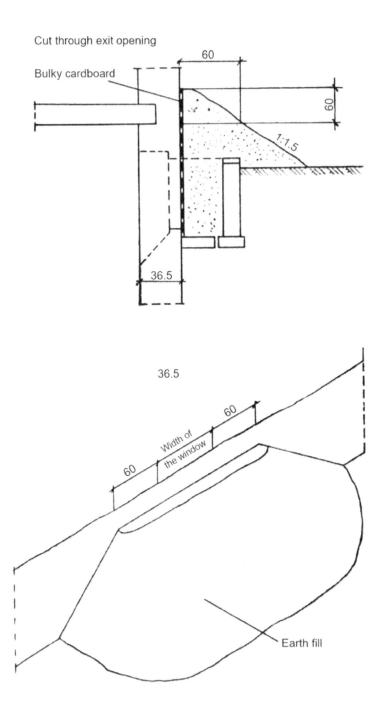

Cut through exit opening

Bulky cardboard

60

60

1:1.5

36.5

36.5

60

Width of
the window

60

60

Earth fill

Fig. 39: Ground fill in the area of the emergency exit

The closure of the window opening can be seen in Figures 40 and 41.

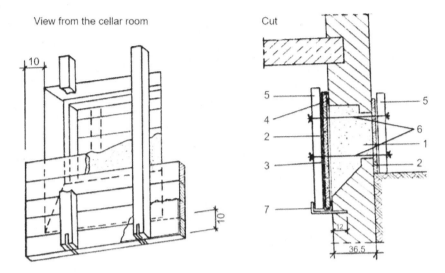

Fig. 40: Closing of window openings located in adjacent rooms of the protective cellar

1. window opening (50 x 37,5) with sand filling, 2. boards (d = 3 cm), 3. foil, paper or similar glued on, 4. felt strips (d = 5-8 mm, b = 3 cm), 5. round timber (8 Ø) or square timber 6/8, 6. bolts for connecting the inner and outer board layers, 7. steel strip (40 x 8 mm) as anchor 12 cm in masonry

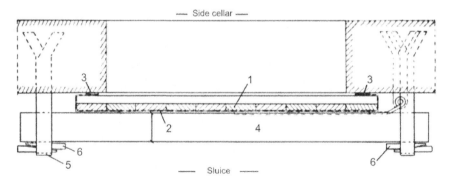

Fig. 41: Closing excess door openings

1. two-ply door leaf (thicknesses according to section 5.33), 2. foil, multi-ply paper or cardboard glued on, 3. felt strips, 4. two squared lumber members (8 x 10 cm) near the door hinges, 5. closed hangers as stone anchors 20 cm in masonry (5 x 1 cm), 6. wedges.

Possible with single-ply door leaf as gas-tight closure.

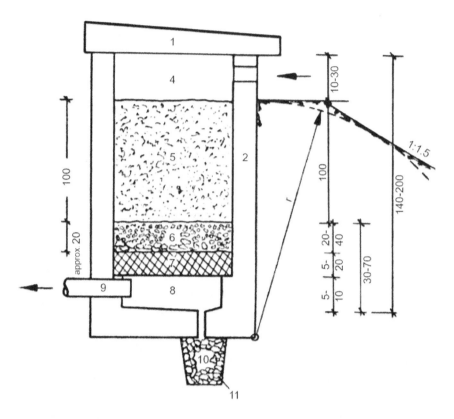

Fig. 42 Basic structure of the coarse sand filter for protective cellar

1. cover plate, 2. filter body, 3. intake opening, 4. air distribution chamber, 5. coarse sand fill, 6. support layer (prevents sand from trickling through), 7. rust according to Fig. 45 or 48, 8. air collection chamber, 9. supply air pipe to protective cellar, 10. condensation drain, 11. stone chunks or coarse gravel

6.3 Water supply, toilets

In the lounge of the shelter there is also a water reserve of 2 1 per person per day (40 persons need 480 litres for 6 days) in containers. Connections to the public water supply must be used as far as possible. If the groundwater level is favourable, it is advisable to install a well with a hand pump in the protective cellar.

It is permitted to set up water flush toilets. In addition, however, a dry toilet with several containers must be installed for every 40 persons. The toilet should be close to the sluice in order to avoid unpleasant smells as far as possible.

In unfavourable cases, water can be forced into the protective structure by the pressure wave through drainage inlets (sinks, lavatories, floor drains). They must therefore be pressure-tight unless a backwater valve has already been installed. Sealing can be carried out by fitting a wooden stopper or by arranging a wooden or metal plate watertight at the opening. These plugs or plates must be secured by bracing against the ceiling (round wood Ø 8 cm), by a load of 30 kg or by a tensile connection (screw connection or similar) so that they are not thrown away by sudden pressure.

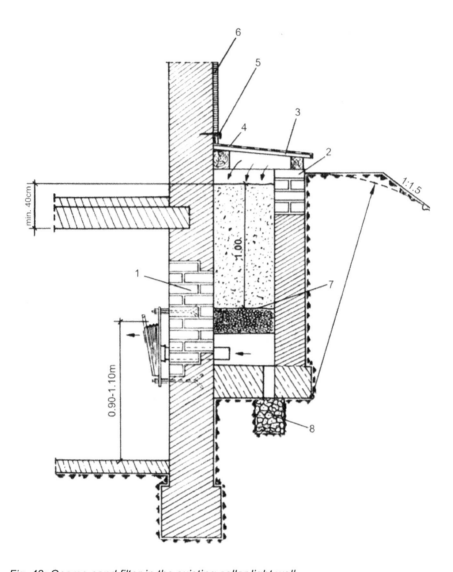

Fig. 43: Coarse sand filter in the existing cellar light well

1. bricked-up window opening. 2. brick lining, 3. cover made of 3 cm thick planks anchored or loaded with tensile strength. 4. roofing felt. 5. wall hooks and cross-cut strip. 6. plaster. 7. filter surface (according to table). 8. stone packing

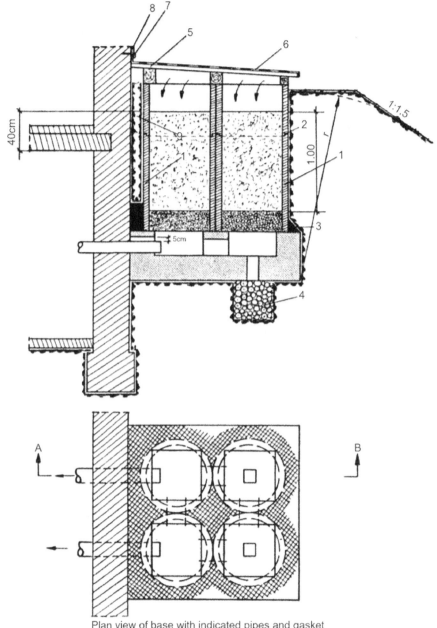

Fig. 44: Coarse sand filter consisting of several round filter bodies outside the building

1. pipes (inner diameter according to Table 12), 2. mortar joint, 3. sealing of concrete, lime or clay mortar, 4. stone packing, 5. covering of at least 3 cm thick boards, 6. roofing felt, 7. wall hooks and capping strip, 8. plaster, 9. fine sand

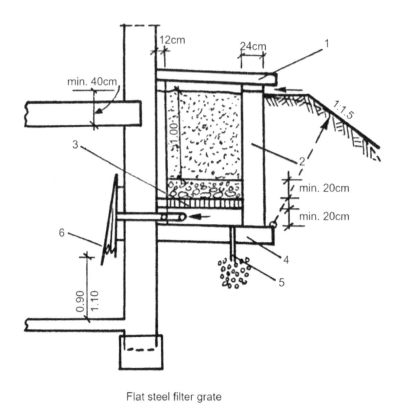

Flat steel filter grate

Dimensions for 1.00m unsupported length in cm

Fig. 45: Coarse sand filter from masonry in front of the outer wall of the building

1. concrete or wood covering, 2. brick in lime cement mortar, 3. steel grid (optionally also brick grid, see Fig. 48), 4. concrete base plate (min. 10 cm thick), 5. steel or clay pipe, 6. bellows fan

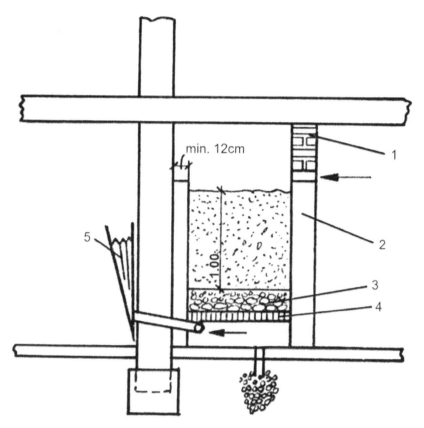

Fig. 46: Coarse sand filter made of masonry in the adjacent cellar room

1st wall pillar for supporting the ceiling (optionally also wooden support),
2. brick in cement mortar (min. 24 cm thick), 3. carrier layer, 4. filter grate according
to fig. 45 or 48, 5. bellows fan

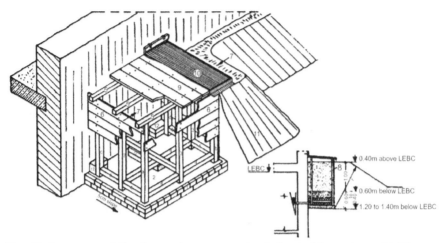

Fig. 47: Coarse sand filter in wooden construction in front of the outer wall of the building

1. base plate made of brick, broken bricks laid in mortar or sand or made of at least 10 cm thick concrete, 2. roofing felt under the entire grate (if necessary only under the stems), 3. stems (at least 12 cm Ø or 10/10 cm) at a maximum distance of 70 cm from each other (for corner stems a and b always use squared lumber, stems c and d minimum distance from the wall 10 cm), 4. expansion timbers (at least 8 cm Ø or 8/8 cm) 15 cm above the base plate, 5. 5. expansion timbers (at least 8 cm Ø or 8/8 cm) 15 cm above the base plate, 5. 5. 5 cm thick concrete roofing felt under the entire grate (if necessary only under the stems), 3. stems (at least 12 cm Ø or 10/10 cm) at a maximum distance of 70 cm from each other (for corner stems a and b always use squared lumber, stems c and d minimum distance from the wall 10 cm). rafters (min. 12 cm Ø or 12/12 cm), 6. lateral formwork made of boards or similar suitable material (sheet metal, reinforced concrete slabs), 7. air inlet opening (min. 100 cm2), 8. roofing felt or Clay (10 cm) or other sealing material on the formwork, 9. covering with 5 cm gradient from planks (min. 3 cm thick), 10. roofing felt or similar waterproof covering, 11. earth fill on the filter, 12. brick or squared timber supports.
Filter grate according to Fig. 48; support layer and coarse sand fill according to Section 6.1.
LEBC = lower edge of basement ceiling

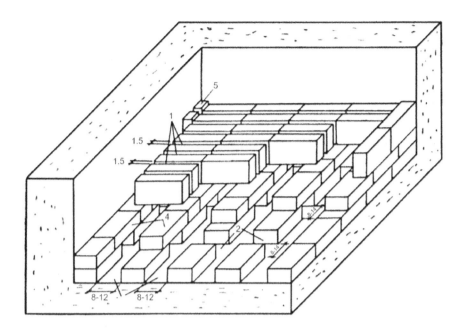

Fig. 48: Filter grate made of solid masonry bricks

1. air gaps (1.5 cm), 2. transverse openings (8-14 cm), 3. row spacing (8-12 cm), 4. bridging the transverse openings with whole stones, 5. wedging each row with lumps of wood or stone

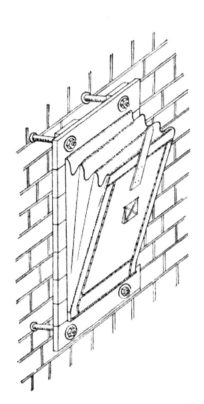

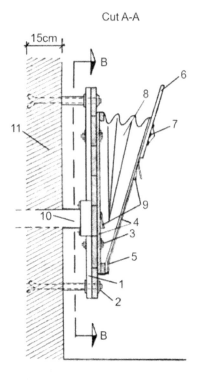

15cm

B

6

8

11

7

9

10

4

3

5

1

2

B

Flap valve for bellows fan

Side view

3 5-6

18   17

15-20

Front view

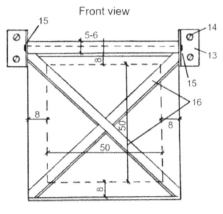

15

5-6

8

14

13

15

16

8

50

8

50

8

Front view   View B-B

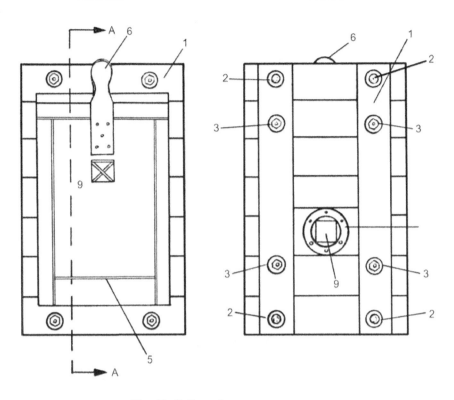

Fig. 49: Bellows fan

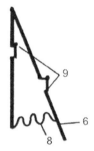

1. wooden panel made of boards (2.4 cm thick), 2. stone screw with sleeve and washer, 3. screw with rubber seal for connecting the bellows fan to the wooden plate, 4. plywood plates, 5. Joint (air mattress fabric glued on and nailed over with narrow leather strips), 6. handle, 7. wood screws, 8. bellows made of air mattress fabric, 9. flap valves, 10. ventilation pipe, 11. wall, 12. flange of the ventilation pipe fastened to the wood moulded piece (4 cm thick) with screws
Flap valve for bellows fan:
12. angle plate, 14. wood screw, 15. nail, 16. glued-on strips (4 mm wide), 17. two glued-on rubber seals, 18. glued joint

If the bellows fan is mounted with the handle downwards, the flap valves must be arranged as shown opposite.

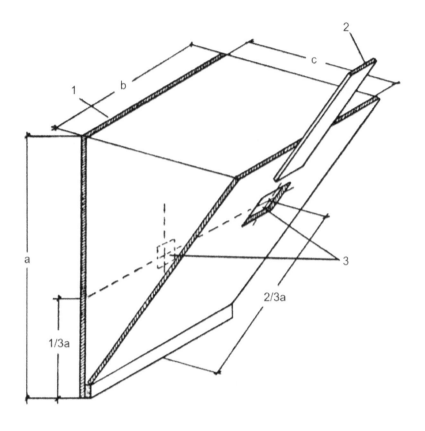

Fig. 50: System sketch of the bellows fan

1. bottom, 2. handle, 3. flap valves
The dimensions of the bellows fan are shown in the following table:

Number of persons in the shelter	a (cm)	b (cm)	c (cm)	Number of strokes required / min
Up to 40	70	45	35	30
40 to 80	100	50	40	30

7. Equipment of a protective cellar for 40 persons

The equipment of the protective cellar must be adapted to the respective local conditions. The following items of equipment are therefore to be regarded as standard values.
Furniture:

- The possibility of lying down for at least one third of the occupants (beds of one to three days, hammocks, tensioned tents, wooden sheds and similar),
- Seats for the remaining occupants (chairs, benches, boxes),
- 1 to 2 small tables (folding boards),
- 1 cupboard or shelf for tools, blankets, bandages, etc.
- Tools and materials:
- 2 shovels,
- 1 cross hoe,
- 1 crowbar (or round steel with tip Ø 30 mm, 1 m long),
- A hatchet,
- 1 Hammer,
- 1 pair of pliers,
- 2 chisels (30 cm long),

1 saw,
Nails, wire, clotheslines, fire extinguishers (if available), extinguishing water, sealing material (such as clay, tow, putty, wooden plugs for pipes, foil, felt strips, etc.), as well as board, plank and beam ends.

Sanitary and medical articles:

- 1 large first aid kit,
- 1 stretcher (makeshift),
  Blankets,
- 1 dry lavatory with several airtight containers and one
  Chlorinated lime container with small blade,
  Toilet paper, Dishwashing detergent and other washing
  powders,
  lockable waste bins.

Food supply:

- Water containers with a capacity of at least 480 litres.
  (If other thirst-quenching drinks are available, this water
  reserve can be reduced by the appropriate amount.)
- Food containers (crates, sacks),
- Catering (per person for about 6 days),
- Hotplate, immersion heater,
- several cooking pots,
- unbreakable crockery.

Protective cellar papers:

- List of house inhabitants,
- Site plan of the own and the neighbouring shelters,
- Attendance book,
- Writing paper.

Other:

- 1 radio receiver,
- Hand lamps and flashlights,
- Candles and lanterns,
- Entertainment material (books, games, toys).

B. PREPARING RADIATION-PROOF SHELTERS

1 Foreword

After Part A describes in detail the measures that must be taken to prepare pressure- and radiation-proof protective cellars, Part B is now intended to provide guidance for the preparation of protective cellars in areas in which direct air attacks are not to be expected. It should be noted that the measures are essentially the same, but there are some differences. For this reason, the following sections refer to the relevant points of Part A, while the deviations are explained in detail.

2 Scope of protection

Cellars in the above-mentioned areas, which are developed according to the principles and instructions described here, offer protection from

- radioactive rays from radioactive fallout and before
- the action of chemical and biological agents.

These shelters must also be equipped and equipped in such a way as to ensure a safe stay for those seeking protection for a period of approximately six days.

3 Selection of suitable rooms

The rooms and installations shown in Figures 51 or 52 should also contain the radiation-proof protective cellars. The same basic requirements as listed in Part A, Section 4 apply to the room sizes.
The selection of the cellar rooms to be extended must be based on the following criteria:

- The rooms should be as underground or at least semi-underground as possible. Rooms above ground level may only be permitted in exceptional cases if their external walls are at least 36.5 cm thick;

- in the case of semi-underground spaces with external walls of buildings less than 36,5 cm thick, the protective cellar wall must be reinforced by earthen embankment or other measures. Terraces, open staircases or similar can be used as already existing reinforcements;

- The protective cellar walls must be designed in such a way that a gas-tight seal can be achieved.

In addition, the aspects mentioned in Part A, Section 4 under serial numbers 2, 3, 4, 5 and 8 must be observed.

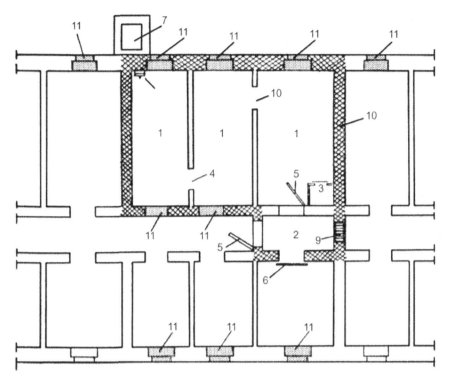

Fig. 51: Lock in the cellar corridor

1. lounge, 2. sluice, 3. dry toilet, 4. wall opening in existing wall, 5. gas-tight door, 6. gas-tight closure, 7. coarse sand filter, 8. bellows ventilator, 9. opening in fire wall, 10. enclosing walls of protective cellar, 11. doors and windows closed gas-tight and radiation-proof

4 Expansion measures

4.1 Reinforcing the walls against the effects of radiation

External protective cellar walls thinner than 36,5 cm shall be reinforced as shown in Figures 4, 5 and 6 to prevent the penetration of radioactive radiation into the protective cellar. The protective measures against the penetration of rainwater must also be taken here, as described in Part A, Section 5.15.

4.2 Entrance

4.2.1 Entrance arrangement

In any case, the entrance should have a sluice which is closed by two gastight doors (to the outside and to the inside) (see Figs. 51 and 52). This sluice must be able to accommodate at least two persons at the same time. A container with chlorinated lime must also be installed here in the cellar corridor in front of the sluice.

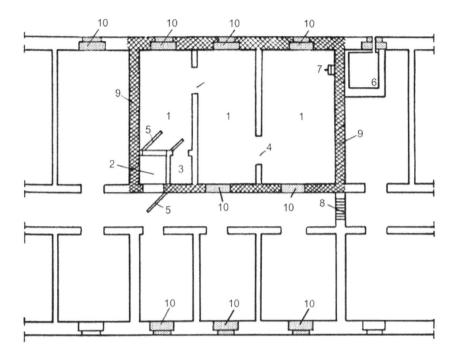

Fig. 52: Protective cellar with sluice in the common room

1. lounge, 2. sluice, 3. dry toilet, 4. wall opening in existing wall, 5. gas-tight door, 6. coarse sand filter, 7. bellows ventilator, 8. opening in fire wall, 9. enclosing walls of protective cellar, 10. gas-tight and radiation-proof closed doors and windows

4.2.2 Sluice

4.2.2.1 Sluice in basement corridor

A sluice in the basement corridor must be arranged in such a way that there are no openings to other cellar rooms in it (see Fig. 51). All openings which are not required are to be closed gas-tight and radiation-proof.

4.2.2.2 Sluice in the common room

For airlocks in the common room, this applies in full, as stated in Part A, Section 5.322.

4.2.3 Doors

4.2.3.1 Gas-tight wooden doors

The two doors must each strike from the outside when viewed from the airlock. The width of the stop is 6 cm. An example of a gas-tight wooden door is shown in Figure 28. The door leaf should be about 2.4 cm thick. Longitudinal and diagonal stiffeners shall be arranged on the side of the doors facing away from the common room. The edge seal of the door is achieved here in the same way as described in Part A, Section 5.331. If there is no masonry stop at the top or bottom edge of the door, it may be made by squared lumber 8/10; 10/10; 8/12; 10/12;.

The sealing between the door leaf and the plaster edge, the gas tightness of the door and the installation of the door hinges is also carried out as described in part A, section 5.3.3.1.

Door latches can be manufactured according to Figure 28, 29 or 41 for the inner door and Figure 53 for the outer door. Each door shall be fitted with two latches, each at the level of the hinges. All anchors must be at least 12 cm in length from the brickwork.

4.2.3.2 Gas-tight steel doors

Any steel door that is not damaged can be used as a gas-tight door. Here, too, only existing steel doors can be used, for which the same requirements apply as in Part A, Section 5.333.

4.3 Connecting passages

If there are several protective cellars in a block of flats, it is recommended to connect them with each other via cellar corridors by creating openings in the fire walls. These openings should be closed again using clay mortar.

4.4 Closing of openings

Unnecessary openings in the enclosing walls of radiation-proof protective cellars are only closed gas-tight and radiation-proof. The pressure-proof closure can be dispensed with as can the splinter-proof closure of window and door openings in rooms adjacent to or opposite the protective cellar.
In addition, the conditions contained in Part A, Section 5.6 for closing openings apply.

5 Technical equipment

5.1 Ventilation

The requirements for the ventilation of radiation-proof protective cellars correspond to those for pressure- and radiation-proof protective cellars. They are shown in Part A, Section 6.1. It should be noted, however, that the filter should not be placed in the cellar if the protective cellar is radiation-proof.

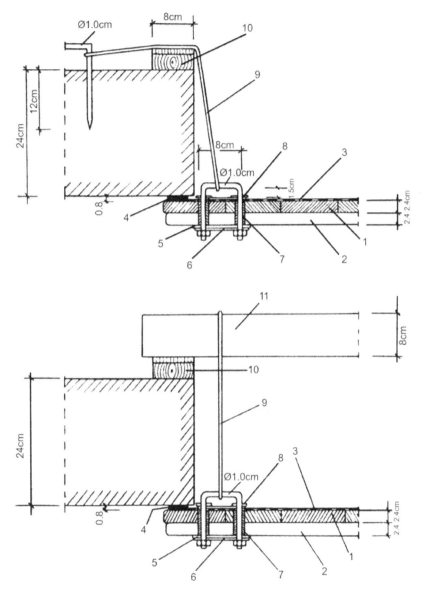

Fig. 53: Closures for external gas-tight door

1st door leaf, 2nd stiffening of the door leaf, 3rd foil or multilayer paper glued on, 4th felt strip, 5th rubber pad, 6th washer, 7th rubber hose, 8th mandrel (4 mm Ø), 9th steel wire rope, 10th double wedge, 11th squared lumber 8/6

5.2 Lighting, electrical energy supply

The requirements for lighting and electrical energy supply in radiation-proof protective cellars correspond to those for pressure- and radiation-proof protective cellars, as can be seen in Part A, Section 6.2.

5.3 Water supply, toilets

The same requirements apply here as in Part A, Section 6.3. However, the measures for sealing drainage inlets described in the last paragraph are omitted.

6 Equipment of a protective cellar for 40 persons

The same specifications in Part A, Section 7 which are to be regarded as guideline values apply to the equipment of the protective cellar.

Disclaimer

The implementation of all information, instructions and strategies contained in this book is at your own risk. The author does not assume any liability for any damage of any kind. Therefore, any legal and compensation claims are excluded. This work was created and written down with the utmost care to the best of my knowledge and belief. The author assumes no responsibility for the topicality, completeness and quality of the work. Misprints and misinformation cannot be completely excluded. For incorrect information provided by the author, no legal responsibility or liability can be assumed in any form

Copyright

Imprint:

Made in United States
Orlando, FL
10 March 2022

15632708R00055